COPYRIGHT:

Reid Reads Publishing

Copyright Katesha D. Reid 2019

All rights reserved. No part of this book may be reproduced in any form without written permission from the author. Reviewers may quote a brief passage for review.

Published 2019

DISCLAIMER

No part of this publication may be reproduced or transmitted in any form or by any means, mechanical or electronic, including photocopying, recording, by any information storage and retrieval system, or transmitted by email without permission in writing from the author.

Neither the author nor the publisher assumes any responsibility for errors, omissions, or contrary interpretations of the subject matter herein. Any perceived slight of any individual or organization is purely unintentional.

Brand and product names are trademarks or registered trademarks of their respective owners.

When I declared that this would be the year of new experiences I never imagined loosing my freedom would be one. I mean I am KD Reid, Freedom Strategist, I am walking boldly in my mission to "Free The People." But none of that matters when unlikely circumstances come to your doorstep or in my case your car door.

So what does 16 hours have anything to do with mindset and freedom? Way more than you can ever have imagined. Let's get started!

1/31/2019 7:00 pm- I was so excited because I had been invited to do a Facebook Live guest appearance on one of my favorite topics "women and freedom." We talked about how women can deal with their emotions in a healthy way so that they can be emotionally free. During this live I also talked about how women needed to be like superman and take off the cape, embracing their inner Clark Kent. See every super hero, at least the ones I know, have an alter ego. This alter ego isn't just to hide their identity it is to protect them, to allow them time to be "off". Women take on a lot of roles and a lot of responsibility within each role some of which was never ours to take on. When I talk about this fascination we have with being strong, independent women who can do it all I am always sure to mention how it is killing us. How it is unrealistic, unfair and definitely unhealthy. When we attempt to be everything to everyone normally the person that is left out is us.

We give ourselves the short end of the stick and we show others how to treat us. So if you have never heard this before write it down, it's my first nugget: **Freedom comes from realizing and accepting that you cannot be everything for everyone.** Even when you feel like you have it all together truth of the matter is you don't. Others around you may be happy and you may be creating more ease in their life but the person that is suffering is you.

After finishing the video my daughter and I loaded the car and headed home. We were both tired and ready to get to the house. As we were talking I saw blue lights behind me, I can't even tell you where they came from, so I pulled over hoping that they were trying to get around us. Just as the lights seemed to come out of nowhere the same can happen with unlikely circumstances. Everything seems to be good and you're only focus is getting from here to there and out of nowhere here comes financial lack, a negative relationship, a toxic friendship or my favorite one-fear. So as I pulled over and put the car into park my daughter, unaware of what was going on, began to get nervous. "What's going on mommy, why are you pulling over?" In the calmest voice I could muster I explained to her that the police were pulling us over but I didn't know why however I was sure everything would be okay. By this time I saw the police walking to the passenger window so I let it down.

1/31/2019 8:00 pm- "Yes sir, how can I help you?" Much like the things that lead us to unlikely circumstances my road home was long and dark. The officer was polite and appeared to be genuinely concerned about the missing headlight and the potential of me noticing a deer or a dog to late as a result. This is 2019 and over the past forever years there have been countless negative, even resulting in death, experiences between people of color and law enforcement so that was something in the back of my mind but with my child in the car I had to make a conscious effort to not allow that to cloud my judgment or affect my presentation. **Many times in life when we are led in the path of an unlikely circumstance it is instinctive to react based on our emotions which may be tied to realistic experiences however it is imperative that we only draw from experiences and knowledge that will help us rather than further hinder us.**

While running my license and writing me a ticket for no insurance the officer was notified that I had a warrant for my arrest. When he asked me about the warrant I was baffled. Now i'm not stranger to a traffic ticket but a warrant? That was news to me. "Let me see what I can do," he said as he walked back to his car. I could sense in his speech and his demeanor that he wanted to let me go and give me the opportunity to handle this matter at a later date and on my own time. However the matter was out of his hands and that option was not permissible.

I know there have been times in your life where what you were facing was confusing to you and even felt unfair. **In those moments the freedom mindset isn't finding a way to avoid the situation or the circumstance but embracing it with the belief that something good will come out of it.**

Once the officer asked me to call my parents to come and get my car and my daughter it hit me that this wasn't going to be a quick traffic stop. I had no interest at that time other than making sure my daughter was okay. "Grandma and granddaddy are coming to get you and the car and mommy has to go and get this situation straightened out. It's going to be okay I promise you." Personally the times I understand God them most are when I'm parenting. So little did I know that in that moment God was demonstrating to me that although we are about to be separated (for lack of a better word), and although this is not how you planned your night to go, I need you to know that everything is going to be okay. I need you to know that you are going to be well taken care of.

1/31/2019 9:00 pm- By now my parents had arrived and spoken with the officer, kind of like when God speaks to the enemy before the tests that we experience. That's my child, do what you need to do so that this situation can be resolved, but take care of her. See God knows every unlikely circumstance we encounter beforehand, and not only does He know about it, He has allowed it. Don't worry it is all for a greater good!

My dad explained what was going to happen and made sure I had everything I needed. Retelling this story and seeing it from a spiritual standpoint has me in tears. As I was handcuffed and put in the back of the police car I can't really recall much that was going through my mind. Honestly I was in a state of shock and the feeling was surreal. I remember repeating to myself - I am actually going to jail. I'm 36 years old and I have never been in jail and today i'm going, wow! The ride to the place where I was going to be transferred was silent and although I was familiar with all the places we were passing this time everything looked different.

What makes a circumstance unlikely is that you never imagined yourself being there, being like that. You never understood people in that situation. You definitely never thought that you would end up with a person like that or purchasing a substance like that or thinking so negatively and self-defeating. Much like my ride things seems similar on the outside, all the surroundings probably even seem the same but internally things couldn't be further from the same. The way you feel, the way you are thinking, everything is so different...so unlikely.

1/31/2019 9:45 pm- My journey started in one county but my warrant being in the next county over required me to be transported to a meeting location where I was moved from one car to another.

During the transfer I was informed what the warrant was for and although it was minor, there were still consequences that I had to face.

The officer in the 2nd car was more talkative and I assume it is because he wasn't with me from the beginning. He was able to tell me that my warrant was for a failure to appear charge. He expressed that he had recently been involved with another person who had the same charge. "They were able to leave after a few hours and get things straightened out. Hopefully it's like that for you, I know this is an inconvenience and you want to get home." More than he knew!

Let me go ahead and tell you that the experience of the other person he was speaking about was not the experience that I had. Often we compare and we allow others to compare our journeys to those of similar journeys. We allow the time frames experienced by others to be a guide for us, a standard if you will for what we feel we should be subjected to. The Jones' started a business and made a 45% profit in only 13 months surely I will to. The bad thing about using someone else's experience for a standard is that when we don't reach it we don't look at the differences as to why, we look at self. We begin to see ourselves as a failure, we begin to beat ourselves down for not doing things "right".

Freedom requires you to let go of the schedule you feel your life should be on and embracing your own journey. In your journey is where you will grow, where you will blossom and where you will help others to embrace their journey. No 2 journeys are alike and to hold your journey to the standard of another is doing yourself a disservice.

I know you may be wondering why I attributed the 2nd officer being less somber because he wasn't with me from the beginning. Think about the people that you meet when you are in the dark places of your life. The people that you didn't know prior to that relationship, that drug usage, that mental health lapse, that unlikely circumstance-- they have no attachment to you, they have no remorse for anything that you are doing and more than likely they aren't invested in you being the best you so when you are going down the road of darkness they aren't sad, disappointed or stopping you. Think about it, let's get real real here. I was sharing with someone recently that when I was in the darkest moment of my life and hanging with people I know I wasn't supposed to be with, smoking and drinking with, they had no sadness or regard for my "real life". **They didn't care that I was a professional, a wife or a mother because they didn't have any attachment to that person.**

When I arrived at the booking location everything became even more uncomfortable and unfamiliar, from the seats to the smells and even the company of those around me.

It was then I realized that this unlikely circumstance was not only jeopardizing my physical freedom but also my mental freedom. I don't know if you have ever lost your mental freedom but I have and once I reclaimed it I vowed never to get to that point again. Right there in the booking cage I went from being in shock to making a decision that I would not break.

I had no control over my physical freedom at that point but I had ALL the control over my mental freedom. In the middle of that uncertainty I begin to affirm myself and recite the few scriptures I do know. I begin to pray and I looked out of the dark, dirty window and imagined I was looking out of the balcony on my favorite cruise. because I know it is important to be in the moment of certain things I did take in everything around me because while I wasn't comfortable and was unsure of what was next, i knew that I needed to remember this moment so I wouldn't have to repeat the lesson.

Many times in life we feel as if we are reliving the same situation over and over and the truth is we are. God has a way of teaching us the same lesson over and over and allowing us to take the same test time after time until we get it. Whatever was going to come out of this, I knew it was something I wanted to get right the first time!

1/31/2019 11:45 pm- Action in the booking department doesn't stop, from my observations I would be confident enough to say that night is where they get the most entertainment. After what seemed like a whole day I was loaded on a van and transferred to women's facility down the street. Upon arrival I was given a bag of toiletries, a blanket and a 2 inch mat, if you can even call it that. As the guard searched for a uniform to fit me I was allowed to sit in the hallway on a bench that was more comfortable than what they had at the booking department.

Now pay attention closely to this part because I am certain this part will help you more than any other nugget in this book. While I was sitting, well at this point laying on the bench I was able to stay in the lobby area as they waited for someone to bring me something to wear. By now the handcuffs were off and I had made me a nice plush pallet on the bench. I had spoken to my family and my daughter was doing well, my husband had been informed what was going on and my dad was making sure the wheels kept moving for everyone including me. See what I didn't mention is that as I was trying on pants they thought would fit I asked what the process was for me going home. I had asked the guy in booking but I wanted confirmation because his response was "you have to wait until tomorrow morning when the court opens" and I was basing the expected answer on what the 2nd police had mentioned about someone in a similar situation being able to go after a few hours-see why comparison is a thief.

The female guard seemed surprised when I told her what I was in for and she was certain I could call my dad and leave that night. Excitedly I called my dad only to be told that he had checked and because of certain circumstances with my case, I could not be released until the next morning.

1/31/2019 12:00 am- When my dad broke the news to me that I wouldn't be able to leave that night and would in fact have to stay it was then the first tears began to fall and they came fast. Up until then I had been in shock, I had been hopeful based on what I heard about someone else. I had been in denial.

That has happened to you right? You've been in denial and then suddenly you could no longer be, suddenly you realize that you haven't let go of the pain of your childhood and that's why your business isn't flourising. Suddenly you realize that you talk a good game but your mindset is fixed and you don't really believe you can do that nor do you feel worthy enough to do that. Freedom comes from acknowledging where you are and what you are dealing with no matter how ugly it is. Only through acknowledgment can you experience true freedom.

2/1/2019 12:45 am- After I hung up with my dad and took the biggest breath and exhale I have ever taken, I went back to my bench. "I can do this, I can lay here for 8 more hours - time does go by fast when you're sleep - I can do this. I mean at least I can just lay here and not behind bars or anything. No one is here but me this is chill.

I didn't realize this huge mindset trap I was falling in until 2 hours later when I was awakened to someone bringing me a shirt. Re-read the previous paragraph again and see if you can find the mistake. We have all made it at one time or another and is huge! **The mistake I made was thinking I was "Free" because I appeared to be "more free" than the other inmates.** In life we often feel like we are free because our circumstances look better than others around us. We can be comfortable in that "fake freedom". Still don't know what i'm talking about- have you ever said "well look at her relationship, mine ain't that bad" "I'm not happy with my job but at least I'm not as miserable as such and such" "I know my life needs fixing but whew, have you seen her life?" Sound familiar? I thought so, we have all had these thoughts at one point or another and the reality is it is faulty and detrimental thinking. **Your life may seem to be better than others around you but the reality is that doesn't take away from the lack of freedom you have in your life.**

2/1/2019 2:45 am- I was instructed to pick up my belongings and choose a cell. I went to the cell she suggested and there was already 3 women in there. 2 on the beds and 1 on the floor. now there were 2 open top bunks but I am a plus size lady who was not about to get on a top bunk. So on the floor I went. I am not exaggerating when I tell you I laid 18 inches from the toilet. Everytime one of my cellmates gor up to use the bathroom I covered my head and turned my face the other way praying that all they had to do was pee. That may have been the prayer I wanted God to answer the most. Something about being in a small living quarter and laying less than 2 feet away from a toilet puts things into perspective in ways they've never been before.

Once I was situated and I heard the door lock, a sound I'll never soon forget, I laid there with my eyes wide open and prayed for God to help me make the best of this circumstance. "Lord," I prayed, "since I'm here can you just give me rest. let me rest in your lap."

2/1/2019 4:45 am- You know that camp music that plays when it is time to wake up. They played that on the loud speaker when it was time to wake up and eat breakfast. Why they serve breakfast so early was beyond me but I did not plan on being there long so I did not ask. People became aware that a new lady was on the unit. They would come by and peep their head in the window. Some would come by and ask me if I was coming out. I shook my head no and to a few I verbally replied "no ma'am."

Although I had been on the unit or block whatever it is called. I had been in this unlikely circumstance for over 7 hours it wasn't until just now that people became aware. Freedom is realizing that sometimes you will be in a place long before others realize that you are there. So often I hear people take on the mindset that no one cares about them because they did not even realize they were in a dark place. What if that person you're blaming and on the verge of cutting off has no idea that you're there. It is not solely up to others to recognize where you are. You have the control to let them know. Now there are times we don't want others to know for various reasons. I get it!

I could have come into the cell making my presence known but I preferred not to. However if that is the route you take please understand that freedom is knowing that everyone that doesn't check on you or help you is not aware that you even need them. Also sometimes the situations we ate in are meant to teach us and everyone who can help us isn't meant to.

2/1/2019 6:45 am- After breakfast everyone went back to their rooms and resumed sleeping. I found myself dozing back off. "Katesha Reid, leave your stuff here and come with me." I was happy they called my name but why was I instructed to leave my stuff behind? Turns out I had not been fully booked in and they needed to get a picture of me. I saw them taking pictures of everyone and I assumed because they had a picture of me from a prior court payment arrangement that I was good. Being brought back here was an inconvenience. It was cold, my clothes were falling off and I had to be back in those wretched handcuffs for transport.

Skipping part of the process only requires that you are inconvenienced at a later time. In the moment it feels like you're being given preferential treatment or shortening your learning curve but on the contrary you're actually setting yourself up for disappointment later down the road. The only benefit to having to go back was that I could see that it was daylight and knew my time there was growing close to and end...or so I hoped!

2/1/2019 7:30 am- When I got back to my cell I immediately went back to sleep. My goal was to sleep as much as I could. My fear was that someone would find out that I was only going to be there until this situation was handled and out of jealousy they would do something to jeopardize my pending freedom.

Earlier I spoke about people who you meet during your dark times not being attached to the person you truly are. Well there are also those who have been in this place longer than you and may not see the end to their pain. The thought of you making it over or through doesn't excite them. Quite the opposite, they are there to keep you from your freedom. They aren't on the path to freedom so why would they help you. This is why it is important for you to know that freedom comes when you no longer feel the need to respond to everyone or everything. Is it tempting, absolutely but when your eyes are on the bigger picture while still remembering how you feel during the unlikely circumstance it becomes easier and necessary.

2/1/2019 9:50 am- I know this may be surprising but I slept really well until I couldn't sleep anymore. As soon as I woke up I I made a call to my dad. What he said was music to my ears. My daughter was doing okay, my other went to school as usual and my ticket and warrant had been paid in full. Now the waiting game started and the tears resumed. Why was I crying you asked.

Although I knew my freedom was coming and I had been assured that I would be released that day there just couldn't be any promises as to a specific time.

Knowing that the end is near but being unsure of when was almost as bad as not knowing what was going on from the beginning.

2/1/2019 10:30 am- Everything was early here. Breakfast at 4:45 and lunch before 11. Again I did not engage in lunch. By this time I had the thought process that I was physically there but mentally I was not. Actually at this point I had started to focus on how I was going to catch up on all of the work I had missed at work and in my business.

Before I hung up with my dad he said something that hit home for me. "You stay strong and do what you gotta do in there and know that things are being handled out here. just lunch served, no participation, no interaction, no response/ things are going on behind the scene on your behalf."

Think about that from a spiritual perspective and a mindset standpoint. How freeing is it to know that all you have to do is handle you, take care of you and everything else is being handled. This is why when I am teaching about mindset and freedom the topic of faith always makes an appearance.

Freedom is having the mindset that if you do what you're called to do, if you follow the dream placed in your spirit then all resources connections and keys to success will be provided to you. Things are being handled behind the scenes.

2/1/2019 11:30 am- "Katesha Reid," I looked around to see where this deep unfamiliar voice was coming from. "Speak into the intercom over there," she said. "Katesha Reid get all your things and head to the exit door." The guard was summoning me and I couldn't be more excited. There was no need to gather anything because I never unpacked anything.

When you finally get to a place where you realize that this is not your final destination you don't get comfortable. You do things to make yourself uncomfortable so you will stay focused. The she I was referring to, the one who told me where the voice was coming from and the one who showed me where the exit was-- was the same cellmate who I overheard talking about me, the same inmate I knew was whispering about me because everyone turned to look. Freedom is not needing to engage anyone, not needing to defend anything and watching as the same person who attacked you have a part in your release!!

2/1/2019 11:45 am- I was transported back to central booking, given a release statement and set free. Funny how the release can be in the same space as the intake but the process isn't as long or as tedious as the intake process.

2/1/2019 12:00 pm- I was officially FREE! 16 hours of my life in jail may not seem like long to you but to me and my family it was an unlikely circumstance that was 16 hours to long. No matter what part you play to find yourself in an unlikely circumstance make sure that you learn the lesson and avoid repeating the mistake.

My freedom was compromised for 16 hours. How long will continue to let yours be?

Hi, I am KD Reid Freedom Strategist, MIndset Coach, Mental Health Professional, Author & Transformational Speaker!

It is my hope and prayer that something I experienced or shared in this book will help you become **forever free**.

Freedom is something that you should not only desire, but you deserve. If you have things in your life you've been dealing with, things you feel are holding you back and things that continue to keep you bound- let's talk!

Visit my website www.thekdreid.com
Follow me on Facebook
www.facebook.com/iamkdreid
Email me at info@thekdreid.com

I look forward to hearing from you!
Be More! Be Bold! Be FREE!!

NOTES

NOTES

NOTES

NOTES

NOTES

Made in the USA
Columbia, SC
06 October 2023